Killer Whales

By Beth Adelman

The
Child's
World®
www.childsworld.com

Published in the United States of America by The Child's World®
P.O. Box 326 • Chanhassen, MN 55317-0326
800-599-READ • www.childsworld.com

ACKNOWLEDGMENTS

The Child's World®: Mary Berendes, Publishing Director

Produced by Shoreline Publishing Group LLC
President / Editorial Director: James Buckley, Jr.
Designer: Tom Carling, carlingdesign.com
Cover Art: Slimfilms
Copy Editor: Beth Adelman

Photo Credits
Cover—Main: Minden Pictures; Bottom: Dreamstime.com (3).
Interior—AP/Wide World: 26; Corbis: 7, 21, 24; Dreamstime.com:
11; Getty Images: 25, 29; Rolf Hecker: 14, 18; iStock: 8, 23; Minden
Pictures: 5, 6, 13, 15

LIBRARY OF CONGRESS CATALOGING-IN-PUBLICATION DATA

Adelman, Beth.
  Killer whales / by Beth Adelman.
    p. cm. — (Boys rock!)
  Includes bibliographical references (p.   ).
  ISBN 1-59296-732-9 (library bound : alk. paper)
  1. Killer whale—Juvenile literature. I. Title. II. Series.
  QL737.C432A34 2006
  599.53'6—dc22
                              2006009022

CONTENTS

KILLER WHALE Basics

You think sharks are the baddest guys in the ocean? Think again! Killer whales are the ocean's super **predators**. They're mammals, the largest, fastest members of the dolphin family. They're strong, smart, and deadly.

They're big, too! Males can be 28 feet (9 m) long and weigh 12,000 pounds (5,443 kg). The females are only a little

smaller—25 feet (8 m) long and up to 8,000 pounds (3,629 kg). Like all dolphins, killer whales have torpedo-shaped bodies that glide smoothly through the water. When these powerful creatures chase a meal, they can go up to 45 miles (72 km) an hour!

The largest killer whale ever found was a male 32 feet (10 m) long and weighing 22,000 pounds (9,979 kg)!

5

A pair of killer whales off the coast of western Canada look to turn these penguins into black-and-white snacks.

Killer whales are found in almost all of the world's oceans. They usually stay in areas where the water is colder. They are seen most often in the Arctic and Antarctic and around Alaska. They also live off the coasts of northwest Canada, northern California, northern Europe, and Greenland.

Even from shore, people can watch wild killer whales doing what they do best— hunting.

Killer whales eat fish, squid, and penguins. They also eat **mammals** such as seals, sea lions, and dolphins.

To help them hunt, killer whales have about 45 cone-shaped teeth. Each is about three inches long and is shaped for ripping and tearing **prey**.

Killer whales can go up on the ice to grab seals. They swallow these cute little guys whole.

Here's a look at a killer whale's eye, plus a good view of its smooth skin.

Like all great hunters, killer whales see and hear very well. Their eyesight is good above and under the water, and they can hear a wide range of sounds. Their skin is very sensitive to touch, too.

What's in a Name?

Another name for the killer whale is *orca*. This name comes from a Latin word that means "whale." The scientific name for the killer whale, *Orcinus orca*, is based on this Latin word.

Killer whales use **echolocation** to find their way and to locate prey underwater. They make sounds like clicks. The sounds bounce off objects, and their echoes return to a special hearing **organ**. Based on how quickly the sound bounces back, the animal can tell what is in front of it and where it is.

All the members of the dolphin family use echolocation to find their way. Bats use it, too.

Killer whales are mammals and give birth to live, air-breathing babies called calves. These are big babies! Newborn killer whales are about 8 feet (2 m) long and weigh 300 to 400 pounds (136 kg to 181 kg)! The calves swim to the surface to breathe.

The calves drink their mother's milk for about a year and a half. Young killer whales often stay with their mothers for 10 years or more. Living in a group helps them learn their fearsome hunting skills.

Like all mammals who live in the sea, killer whales must come to the surface to breathe. They breathe through a blowhole on top of their head.

How can you tell males from females? Look at the **dorsal** fin—the fin that sticks up on the whale's back. Often, males have a very tall dorsal fin shaped like a triangle. It can be six feet (2 m) tall. Most females' dorsal fins are only about three feet (1 m) tall and are curved.

Here's a mom and her calf. Female killer whales usually have one calf every three to ten years.

2

A KILLER WHALE'S Life

Killer whales live in groups called **pods**. There are usually about five to 30 animals in a pod. "Superpods" of 100 killer whales have also been spotted. A pod is like a family, and some pods stay together for many years.

Pods do everything together, including traveling and hunting. Sounds make it easier for the pod members to live and work together. They use whistles, buzzing sounds, and screeches. Each pod has its own style of calls. This language helps the members feel like a family.

Scientists who study killer whales in the wild can tell which pod is nearby just by listening to the calls the whales make.

Most pods of killer whales are led by females. Here's a group swimming along the coast of Canada.

Not all pods hunt the same way. The members of each pod learn and develop their teamwork in hunting.

Killer whales are such successful hunters because all the animals in the pod work together. For example, pod members sometimes force lots of fish into one area and then take turns feeding. In other cases, the members join forces to surround a larger animal, such as a blue whale. They wear the animal down until it becomes a meal.

Killer whales have other ways of catching their prey. Sometimes they smack into the bottom edge of a small piece of floating ice. The sudden blow can knock a resting seal into the sea! Sometimes a killer whale will actually slide up out of the water and onto a beach to grab an animal.

The Food Chain

Ocean mammals and big fish eat smaller fish. Those fish eat even smaller fish, who eat even tinier creatures. This list of animals that eat other animals is called the *food chain*. Killer whales are on the top of the ocean food chain.

Killer whales are also awesome **acrobats**. Big adults often "breach," throwing themselves up out of the water in splashing body twists. When they're "spyhopping," they pop their heads and upper bodies up from the waves and swim backwards. They also slap their tail fins or dorsal fins on the water, making a loud sound.

Scientists think these acrobatics are the animals' ways of expressing their feelings. They might be showing feelings of excitement or anger. They might even be inviting others to play. Scientists think spyhopping might be a way of looking around, since killer whales often do this when boats get close.

This killer whale is "breaching," or leaping out of the water off the coast of Washington state.

Hey, what's up? These killer whales are spyhopping to see what's going on at the surface.

People in different families, communities, and countries often have different ways of behaving. Killer whale pods in different areas have different ways of behaving, too.

Some killer whales live in large groups. Others travel in smaller groups, and members of the group come and go. Others live far out at sea, and scientists don't know much about those groups. The different kinds of killer whale groups have their own ways of hunting and communicating, and places they like to go.

One important part of being in a pod is working together. Teamwork often brings more food. For example, near Norway, killer whales herd schools of herring into tight balls of fish. After **stunning** the herring with smacks of their tails, the killer whales swoop in to eat them.

An average-sized killer whale can eat 500 pounds (227 kg) of food every day!

These differences aren't just about eating, either. In the Crozet Islands, between Antarctica and South Africa, the killer whales visit **kelp** beds. Several times a day, they swim through the long, thick strands of seaweed. They don't eat anything while they're in the kelp beds. They just seem to like the feeling of swimming through them. There are kelp beds off the coast of northern California, too. But the killer whales who live there don't swim in them at all.

Kelp is a kind of seaweed. It grows so tall that that bunches of it are usually called a "kelp forest."

Killer whales in British Columbia, Canada, like to rub themselves on shallow, pebbly beaches. Other killer whales who live near beaches don't do this.

Sunlight slips through the leafy green stalks of a kelp forest, where some killer whales like to swim.

3

KILLER WHALE
Stories

People all over the world have told tales about the awesome power of killer whales. To some groups of people, the killer whale is a helpful animal. To others, it is a fierce predator. In the Pacific Northwest, killer whales are important to many groups of people. The Haida (HI-dah) people viewed killer whales as members of a race of powerful beings who live in the ocean.

Totem poles use images to tell important stories. This story features a killer whale.

Tlingit people tell a story about how a man carved the first killer whale from a piece of wood. In Tlingit beliefs, killer whales are the protectors of the ocean.

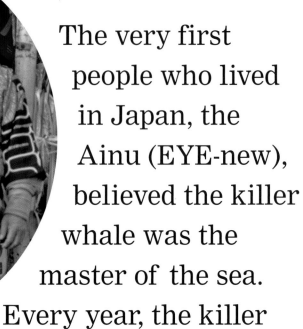

Some Ainu people show their traditional clothing. The designs are based on the shapes of killer whales and other creatures.

The very first people who lived in Japan, the Ainu (EYE-new), believed the killer whale was the master of the sea. Every year, the killer whale sent his friends, the salmon, up streams to visit the Ainu and the human world. Some of the salmon allowed themselves to be eaten by people. Other salmon swam back to report to the mighty killer whales on how well the humans had welcomed them.

People in other parts of the world tell stories about killer whales, too. Most of these places are near the coastlines where killer whales live. Inuit people in Alaska tell tales of Akhlut, a killer whale who could turn into a wolf and walk on land.

Killer Whales on Ice

As part of their team logo, the Vancouver Canucks hockey team wears a killer whale in the shape of a C. One of the reasons is that many killer whales live off the coast of Vancouver, Canada.

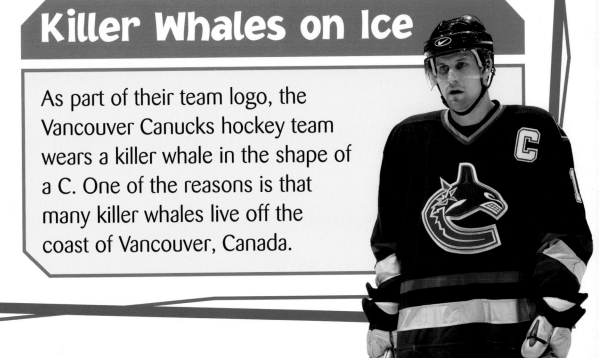

Killer whales have also been movie stars. The most famous was Keiko, who starred in the 1997 movie *Free Willy*. In this family-friendly movie, a boy who lost his mother makes friends with a killer whale at an amusement park.

Keiko was freed from this marine park in Mexico.

The animal also lost his family when he was captured, so he and the boy have something in common. When the animal's life is threatened, the boy saves him by helping him escape to the ocean.

In real life, Keiko was living in a Mexican **marine park** in a tank that was too small. After he became a movie star, many people worked together to help him return to the wild ocean. Keiko did return to the ocean, but sadly, died soon after.

Movies are cool, but the best place to see killer whales is in the ocean. You might be lucky enough to live someplace where killer whales swim near shore. Or maybe you'll see them when you're on vacation. Special boat rides often take visitors to places where they can see killer whales swimming free.

If you can't get to a place where wild killer whales live, the next best thing is to see them in marine parks and **aquariums**.

If you're a seal, killer whales are fierce and deadly enemies. If you're a human, however, killer whales are amazing creatures to learn about. Few animals combine speed, size, and intelligence the way they do.

Up, up, and away! A killer whale shows her stuff at SeaWorld. Marine parks like this are located in many cities in the U.S. and Canada.

GLOSSARY

acrobats   people or animals that are good at gymnastics moves such as jumps and flips

aquarium   a place or a tank where people can look at animals that live in the water

dorsal   on or near the back, such as a dorsal fin

echolocation   the ability to use sounds and their echoes to find your way or find food

kelp   a kind of seaweed that grows in long, thick strings and can form a dense underwater "forest"

mammals   warm-blooded animals that breathe air, give birth to live babies, and feed them milk from their bodies

marine park   a special kind of zoo that has animals that live in the ocean

organ   a part of the body that is not bone or muscle and that has a special job

pods   groups of killer whales that live together like a family

predators   animals that eat other animals

prey   an animal that is food for other animals

stunning   making an animal unable to move, such as by hitting it hard

FIND OUT MORE

BOOKS

Killer Whales
by Mark Carwardine
(DK Publishing, New York) 2002
This book has tons of great photos and fun facts about killer
whales and how they live.

Killer Whales
by Sandra Markle
(First Avenue Editions, Minneapolis, MN) 2003
A science writer takes a close-up look at killer whales and how
they behave.

Orcas Around Me
by Deborah Page
(Albert Whitman Co., Morton Grove, IL) 1997
A story about a fishing boat and how it works around killer
whales.

Whales Passing
by Eve Bunting
(Blue Sky Press, New York) 2003
A story in which a boy and his father watch and learn about
killer whales.

WEB SITES

Visit our home page for lots of links about killer whales and other
marine mammals: www.childsworld.com/links

Note to Parents, Teachers, and Librarians: We routinely check our Web links to
make sure they're safe, active sites—so encourage your readers to check them out!

INDEX

Beth Adelman writes about and edits books about animals. She has won several awards from the Cat Writers Association and the Dog Writers Association of America and is currently on the board of directors of the International Association of Animal Behavior Consultants. One of her favorite travel activities is visiting aquariums and zoos around the world. She has also been lucky enough to see wild killer whales in Alaska.